Meetings, Memes And Melted Ice Cream

Smiling Through The Chaos

Mahitha Choudhary

BookLeaf Publishing

India | USA | UK

Made with ❤ on the BookLeaf Publishing Platform
www.bookleafpub.in
www.bookleafpub.com

Dedication

To my Father,
who handed me my first book
and unknowingly sparked a lifelong love for them.
Thank you for reading my tiny letters—
even the ones demanding an apology from you at age
six.
Your quiet encouragement made me a reader,
and your love made me brave enough to become a
writer.

Preface

Hi there.

This book was born somewhere between work calls, baby naps, laundry piles, and snack runs. It wasn't crafted in a quiet cabin in the woods or with an inspiring view—but somewhere much more chaotic: real life.

By day, I work in IT, trying to keep things from falling apart (or at least not letting them crash too loudly). By night—or more realistically, during unpredictable nap windows—I write about the wonderfully absurd mess that is modern adulthood.

If you're wondering what Meetings, Memes, and Melted Ice Cream means, it's basically adulthood in three acts: Meetings represent the never-ending to-do lists, the Zoom fatigue, and the corporate chaos we're all quietly screaming through.
-Memes are the glue holding our sanity together—barely.
-And melted ice cream? That's the emotional state. The moment your treat melts before you can enjoy it— because life, responsibilities, and maybe a screaming toddler got in the way.

This book is for anyone who's ever opened their inbox in quiet dread, turned laundry folding into a motivational speech, or tried to "live in the moment" while reheating coffee for the third time. I hope these poems give you a reason to smile, nod knowingly, and feel a little less alone.

Let's turn the page and smile through the chaos together.

(Note: All characters and situations are fictional or dramatized for humor. Any resemblance to real coworkers, meetings, or snack hoarders is purely coincidental. No actual office chairs were harmed in the making of this book.)

—Mahitha

Acknowledgements

To my parents—

Papa, who first introduced me to the magic of books and poems

and Mom, whose strength, love, and quiet encouragement continue to echo in everything I do.

Thank you for teaching me to be brave and for always cheering me on—even when my hobbies got a little weird.

To my loving family—

thank you for standing behind me (and beside me and occasionally dragging me forward).

Your unwavering support means the world—even when I was obsessing over one comma for three hours.

To my friends, you know who you are—

we dreamed this up over endless chats and "someday" conversations. Turns out someday is today, and I couldn't have done it without your hype, honesty, and memes.

To my publisher—

thank you for turning my late-night ramblings into something beautifully real. You made my dream of becoming a writer come true.

And finally, to you dear reader—
thank you for picking up this book, flipping through the pages, and sharing a smile along the way.

With Love
Mahitha

1. When I Grow Up

I swore I'd be an Astronaut Queen,
With laser boots and jelly bean sheen.
I'd ride a comet to outer space,
And own a moon house with parking space.
Or maybe a Pirate with rainbow hair,
Who sailed on juice waves without a care.
I'd find lost gold and pet a shark,
and never wake up before it's dark.
A Pop Star? Sure! With glitter mic,
My songs would rule- even dad would like.
I'd tour the world in sparkly boots,
And sign my name on pizza toots.
But somehow now I pay my bills,
Answer emails, fight laundry hills.
No dragons, rockets, or treasure maps
Just meetings and... "Please see attached."
Still, sometimes when I daydream deep,
That Pirate Princess starts to creep.
And though I'm not in space (yet, my friend),
I still chase stars, just with a pen.

2. The Adulthood Scam

As kids we thought, "Can't wait to grow!
No bedtime rules, no 'no' means no!"
We dreamed of snacks and staying up late—
Not taxes, chores, and interest rates.
They never warned us bills can bite,
That socks go missing every night.
You clean one room, then blink—it's gone,
Now your laundry pile has spawned a spawn.
You said, "I'll eat cake for every meal!"
Now fiber is important to seals the deal.
"Let's travel the world!" your heart once said—
But your wallet just laughed and went to bed.
You thought your boss would be like cool shows—
Instead it's just emails and "no-no-no"s.
You spend your days in coffee loops,
And nights attending Tupperware groups.
Yet somehow still, we call it fine—
With half-dead plants and boxed-up wine.
We text "adulting" like we're pros,
And secretly Google: "Do I need more pillows?"

3. New Year, Gym Fantasy

January came, I made a vow:
"This year I'll lift! I'll sweat! Somehow!"
I bought new shoes, some stretchy gear—
Then sat and snacked for half the year.
I joined a gym. I paid upfront.
My bank account pulled one big stunt.
I walked in once, all pumped with pride...
Then saw the weights and almost died.
Treadmills stared with judging lights,
While gym bros grunted into heights.
I stretched. I squeaked. My leg gave out—
Then faked a phone call. "Gotta bounce!"
I tried again the very next week,
My motivation? Mild and bleak.
Ten jumping jacks, then water break—
And twenty minutes scrolling "cake."
So now I pass the gym each day,
Wave at the door, then walk away.
"New Year, New Me"? That ship has sailed—
But at least my snack goals never failed.

4. I Work Out (My Stress)

I don't lift weights—I lift regret,
I carry panic like a pet.
My treadmill is a mental loop
That runs on dread and snack food soup.
Crunches? Sure, I crunch on chips.
Stretching? When life tightens its grips.
Cardio comes when I panic and flee—
From tasks, emotions, and responsibility.
I sweat when emails start to yell,
When plans implode or printers smell.
My fitness goal? Just stay upright,
And maybe scream into the night.
Yoga? I tried. I bent, I cracked.
My spine and I made no pact.
Meditation made me nap—
That counts, right? A mindful trap.
So yes, I work out every day,
But not in any normal way.
My muscles ache from dodging doom
Emotionally fit. You're welcome, Zoom.

5. Morning Person: No!

I planned my morning, crisp and bright,
To rise before the crack of light.
Set soothing chimes to ease the blow—
Still woke at noon, face in a throw.
I pictured yoga, toast, and sun,
Instead, I grunted, "Nope. We're done."
My blanket clung with ninja might—
Roundhouse kicked me into night.
I stumbled out, a caffeine ghost,
Burned my toast and missed my oats.
The birds chirped loud with zero shame—
While I just glared and cursed their name.
I tried again the next day too—
Lit candles, made a greenish goo.
Still hit snooze like striking gold,
Then woke up cranky, tired, and cold.
Morning folks, I tip my hat.
Your sunrise joy? I'm not like that.
You rise and glow. I rise and whine—
Some of us just peak post–dinner time.

6. Dear Alarm Clock

You scream at me before the dawn,
With tones that sound like chaos spawn.
I dream of smashing your plastic face,
But sadly, you're plugged in... in place.
You never ask if I slept okay,
Just beep and buzz and ruin my day.
You don't care if I need more sleep—
You wake me like a haunted sheep.
I've hit snooze more than I should,
But you keep coming like no friend would.
I beg for peace, I plead for rest—
But you don't stop. You're on a quest.
One day I'll rise without your call,
I'll burn your cord, I'll free us all.
Until that day, I weep, I whine—
My soul is yours at 6:09.
So dearest clock, let's make this clear:
You bring me nothing but dread and fear.
I hope you trip on your own sound,
And fall deep into lost-and-found.

7. Monday, you Monster

Monday, oh Monday, you sneaky old creep,
You stole my weekend, my snacks, and my sleep.
I opened my eyes, the sun said "hooray!"
But my inbox just screamed, "It's Judgment Day."
Fifty-five emails, not one says "hi",
Just "circle back", "urgent", and "please reply".
One says "per my last"—oh no, not again,
The passive-aggression is strong in this pen.
I sip on my coffee, it tastes like despair,
My to-do list grows while I just sit and stare.
Janet wants updates, Bob wants a chart,
And I just want tacos and a brand-new start.
The weekend was lovely, I slept and I danced,
Now I'm in a Zoom call where no one's advanced.
"Can everyone mute?" "You're still on mute!"
This could've been an email… I'm not being cute.
Monday, you trickster, you corporate clown,
You drag my soul down, down, down.
But I'll fake a smile, I'll play the part—
While Googling jobs that involve zero charts.

8. Water Cooler Walk

I left my desk, so calm, so pure—
To fill my bottle, hydrate, be sure.
A quick two minutes, that was the goal…
Then Susan appeared. Down went my soul.
"Did you watch the thing last night?"
She asks with joy and way too light.
I nod politely, trapped mid-hall—
While Dave joins in, uninvited call.
Then Lisa showed up from HR,
With tales about her toddler's jar.
The hallway buzzed, snacks made the round—
My bottle's empty. I just frowned.
I tried to leave, I really tried—
But Mark had thoughts he hadn't tied.
And soon we're deep in caffeine lore—
Desk chairs, pets, and office floor.
By the time I reached the sacred sink,
I'd aged. I'd had too much time to think.
All for hydration, crisp and clean…
Next time, I'll drink from the vending machine.

9. Lunch Thief Tale

I packed it nice—a gourmet feast,
Leftovers from my weekend beast.
I labeled it with name and glare,
"My lunch. Touch this, if you dare."
But when noon came, I danced with glee,
To find... an empty space where it should be.
My salad, gone. My dreams? Betrayed.
Some fridge bandit had snack-slain my day.
I launched a search like Sherlock Holmes,
Checked every desk, the breakroom zones.
But no one cracked, just blank-faced nods—
"Who'd steal your lunch?" (These snack-faced frauds.)
Next day, I packed a decoy meal—
A trap of spice and ghost-pepper zeal.
They struck again. I heard a shout.
And smiled as justice burned its route.
So heed this tale, oh hungry crew:
The fridge is not your tasting zoo.
Respect the label, don't be bold—
Or face revenge... served hot and cold.

10. PowerPoint Daydreams

The lights go dim, the slide appears,
Another meeting, bring on the tears.
"Today we'll cover synergy goals!"
(Meanwhile, my brain just quietly rolls.)
The presenter clicks—slide 1 of 58,
I whisper a prayer, accepting my fate.
Graphs are flying, charts galore,
Someone sneezes, I start to snore.
My eyes are open, my soul is gone,
I'm riding a llama through a pastel dawn.
The spreadsheet turns into a chocolate cake,
And Steve from finance is now a snake.
"Next slide, please"—a dreadful sound,
Yanks me back to corporate ground.
There's bullet points in Comic Sans—
Somewhere, a designer cries into their hands.
They ask for questions—I pretend to write,
Just doodling stars with all my might.
If thoughts could fly, I'd already be gone—
But this PowerPoint? It goes on and on...

11. Looking Busy 101

Step one: open Excel, but don't touch a thing,
Just furrow your brow like you're solving world bling.
Type nonsense in cells, then lean back and sigh,
As if you're decoding the secrets of the sky.
Step two: walk fast with papers in hand,
Even if they're blank, folks will think it's grand.
Add a slight nod, say "Q4's a mess,"
People won't question—just blame the stress.
Step three: set up a meeting with just yourself,
Name it "strategic" and sit like an elf.
Stare at your screen with your AirPods in,
Pretending to lose... or silently win.
Step four: the classic—click-clack on the keys,
Even if it's just typing "I want cheese."
Keep switching tabs from memes to reports,
Alt-tab is the savior of all office sports.
So there you go—my ultimate guide,
To fake the grind while coasting the tide.
Look busy, stay chill, and don't break a sweat,
You've earned that snack—you just haven't moved yet.

12. A Love Letter to My Bed

Dear Bed, my beloved, my blanket-wrapped light,
I think of you always, from morning till night.
While I sit here, stiff-backed, in ergonomic despair,
Your memory whispers from soft, fluffy air.
I miss how you hold me, with pillows so kind,
While this chair pokes my spine like it's lost its mind.
You never judge me for sleeping past ten,
But this cubicle? It's a padded pen.
Oh, how I long for your blanket cocoon,
Instead of this screen and these emails of doom.
You smell like dreams and unbothered grace—
While this chair smells like... sadness and office space.
We had such good times—remember that nap?
Before work stole me with its scheduling trap?
Now I must smile through back-to-back calls,
While you wait for me down the hallway walls.
One day, sweet Bed, I'll return to your side,
To flop like a starfish, with dignity and pride.
Until then, I suffer in this chair's cruel clutch—
Missing your hugs. Missing you. Very much.

13. Friday: The Light

The sun is brighter, the mood feels right,
Even Karen's jokes don't start a fight.
My inbox pings—I almost care—
But it's Friday, friend. I'm halfway there.
The coffee hits just extra strong,
I hum a tune, nothing feels wrong.
My to-do list? A mild suggestion.
My brain? Out of office—no further question.
Lunch turns long, the chats get deep,
We bond, we laugh—we barely peep
At charts or decks or urgent tags...
Just memes and dreams and Friday flags.
That 4 PM glow? Pure delight.
We've mentally left by 12 last night.
We're planning snacks, not next week's task—
And dodging "quick calls" like it's a masked ask.
So cheers to Friday, queen of days,
We've come to the end of maze.
The inbox closes, we're on the run—
Now pass the snacks—the week is done!

14. I Miss My Commute

Ah yes, the traffic, such a delight—
A two-hour crawl at morning light.
I could be working, focused, free...
Instead, I'm stuck behind a tree.
At home, I'm sharp by 8:05,
Emails cleared, caffeine alive.
No awkward chats near the printer stand—
Just deep work done with snacks in hand.
You say "return" like it's a prize,
But pants at 7? That's a crime.
My output's fine, my tasks are met—
I just don't thrive in fluorescent sweat.
I Zoom, I plan, I crush my goals,
No hallway noise, no snack patrols.
I don't need badge scans to commit—
Just Wi-Fi strong and a comfy sit.
So no, dear boss, I won't pretend
That cubicles make teamwork blend.
I work just fine without the drive—
And guess what? My plants agree. High five.

15. The Wi-fi Went Out

The Wi-Fi died without a sound,
My jaw dropped fast—pure panic found.
No memes, no chats, no Netflix stream,
Just offline life? A wild dream.
I wandered out to find a tree,
A bird flew by and looked at me.
The sun was bright, the sky was blue—
I wasn't sure what humans do.
I pet a dog, I kicked a rock,
I even glanced at a ticking clock.
I blinked and thought, "Is this... the sun?"
Then sprinted home like, "That was fun."
The Wi-Fi came back—my soul returned,
I hugged my phone, my fingers burned.
But nature's nice, I will admit...
Still, I need my memes to properly sit.
So here's to Wi-Fi, my glowing gate,
To every click and loading fate.
I may explore once in a while—
But screens, not trees, bring me that smile.

16. Judgy Houseplants

I bought them small, with hope and flair,
I whispered dreams into their air.
"Just sunlight, water, love," they said—
Now they just glare at me instead.
The cactus sighs, the fern looks sad,
The peace lily's low-key kinda mad.
I missed a day? Or maybe eight—
Now photosynthesis won't relate.
They lean away when I walk by,
One even drooped like, "Nice try."
They know I meant well—truly, I did—
But they've seen things I'd rather hid.
I tried to spritz, to sing, to save,
But one plant straight-up dug a grave.
My window garden dreams are done—
Apparently, dirt doesn't equal fun.
Yet still they sit, my leafy crew,
Plotting revenge in pots of dew.
They judge me hard—but they're not wrong.
Plant care is hard. Those TikToks? Wrong.

17. Time Flies Scrolling

I'll just check one post, I said,
While lying cozy in my bed.
But one meme led to twenty more—
Then somehow I was deep in lore.
A dog danced, then a cat made toast,
I liked a reel, then stalked a ghost.
I found a thread on ancient shoes—
Then watched ten hacks I'll never use.
A stranger's lunch, a raccoon fight,
A "day in life" in Bali (right?).
My thumb just moved, my brain checked out—
Yet somehow I know grandma's gout.
Then TikTok whispered, "Just one more."
I blinked, and three hours out the door.
My phone was hot, my eyes were fried,
Then the sun came up and the night had died.
So here I lie, both shamed and proud,
A scroll survivor, phone-faced, wowed.
Who needs to sleep or read or live—
When dopamine's just one swipe give?

18. Snacks, Spirit Animal

Some say their spirit is strong or wise,
A wolf, an eagle, with noble eyes.
But deep in my soul, what do I see?
A bag of chips just staring at me.
Cookies call louder than destiny's voice,
Popcorn crackles like it made the choice.
My willpower? Missing. My desk drawer? Stuffed.
With treats and sweets and crackers puffed.
Then comes ice cream, the crown of delight,
With sprinkles that dance in the freezer's cold light.
A pint of peace in a world gone mad—
Even deadlines pause when it's mint chocolate bad.
Stress? Have a pretzel. Bored? Here's some cheese.
Big scary meeting? Two scoops, please.
My brain may lag, my plans may sink—
But give me ice cream and I'll start to think.
If snacks were a language, I'd be fluent and proud,
A sugar-salt symphony playing out loud.
So judge me not when I crunch mid-Zoom—
My spirit animal's busy... and it brought a spoon.

19. Pizza, My Second Love

Oh pizza box, you sweet surprise,
With melted cheese and carb-filled highs.
You never judge, you never stray—
Just show up hot and save the day.
Your crust is warm, your center gooey,
You're loyal, round, and always chewy.
Toppings? Wild. From plain to bold—
Even pineapple (yeah, I said it. Be cold).
I've ditched real plans to stay with you,
You never ghost or say, "We're through."
You're there at parties, tears, and dates—
You even understood my snack soulmates.
Deep dish, thin crust, folded, flat—
I've loved you fiercely—no shame in that.
You've seen my worst, still stuck around—
Through Netflix binges and midnight rounds.
So here's my truth, no need to shove:
You'll always be my saucy love.
And if someday I fall again—
You'll still be there... my cheesy friend.

20. Travel, Bank Says "No!"

I made a list: Greece, Japan, Peru,
A beach, a hike, a mountain view.
I googled flights, I packed in dreams—
Then checked my bank... it stifled screams.
My balance said, "Girl, stay in bed."
"You want a plane? Try walk instead."
"Adventure's fun—but not for you—
Enjoy this brochure from 'Couch View.'"
I watched influencers eat croissants,
While I sat in crumbs and Netflix fonts.
My "passport" now is just a snack,
And I "visit" France through Google Maps.
I tried to budget, really I did,
But rent and coffee robbed the kid.
Now my suitcase holds just hope,
And three socks, and expired soap.
Still, one day soon, I'll board that flight,
With coins I've saved from every night.
But 'til then, dreams cost zero bucks—
And my bank can kindly wish me luck.

21. Parenting The Dictator

They wake at dawn with battle cries,
Demanding waffles—no compromise.
Then suddenly it's toast they need—
Cut in triangles. Not rectangles. Please.
They sprint through rooms half-dressed, mid-yell,
Leave goldfish crumbs where sanity fell.
Their logic? Flawed. Their will? Iron.
They'll wear one sock, and be a lion.
I bribe with snacks, I plead, I sing—
But toddlers fear not anything.
Except... the word "no"—that's war declared.
Prepare the snacks. And dragon lair.
They hug with love that melts your face,
Then bite you mid-embrace, with grace.
One minute sweet, the next a storm—
And you're apologizing to a stuffed unicorn.
Still, in their chaos, there's wild gold—
Tiny hands, big hearts, laughs uncontrolled.
It's hard, it's loud, it's sticky art—
But I'd follow that dictator with all my heart.

22. My Sock Disappeared

I had two socks, a perfect set,
They'd cuddle up, they'd never fret.
But laundry came, and fate grew cold—
Now one is gone. A tale retold.
I checked the drum, I checked the floor,
Behind the couch, beneath the door.
I begged the dryer, "Give it back!"
But it just hummed and stayed on track.
Did it escape to find new feet?
Did it get tired of smelly heat?
Is there a club where single socks go,
To dance and vibe with laundry woe?
Now one remains, a solo friend,
Mismatched forever, fashion's end.
Its partner gone, its soul confused,
And I, the human, feeling used.
So if you find a lonely sock,
Give it a hug and gently talk.
Tell it I searched both far and wide—
Its partner's gone, but it still has pride.

23. Monopoly: Ruins Lives

It starts off calm—we're full of cheer,
"Let's play a game!" (our first mistake, dear).
We set the board, roll dice with grace,
Then battle begins for Boardwalk's space.
I buy some roads, collect some rent,
Someone's in jail—time well spent.
I land on "Chance," it gives me debt,
While I bet Becky owns half the planet.
Then trades get shady, eyes turn cold,
We form alliances, break them bold.
"Mortgage your soul!" someone declares,
As I try not to flip three plastic chairs.
The banker's cheating (I just know),
The thimble cries, "Please let me go."
Someone lands on hotels—twice in a row—
Now they're broke, and it's a soap opera show.
Four hours in, no end in sight,
Our snacks are gone, we've seen the light:
This game's not fun, it's capitalist doom—
But we'll play again. Next Friday. Same room.

24. Fan of Horror Movies

I press play like I'm super brave,
Heart on my sleeve, soul in a grave.
"It's just a film," I smugly say—
Then flinch when popcorn pops my way.
A creak? A knock? My cat walks by?
I scream like someone's about to die.
I pause and squint—what did I see?!
Oh great, now my lamp's haunting me.
The music swells, the lights go dim,
Why is the hallway always grim?
The ghost appears, the doll just moved—
I suddenly need all doors removed.
I check the locks, I hug my knees,
I side-eye every swaying tree.
Then someone texts, "Behind you, bro!"
And that's how I became a burrito.
Still, next week, I'll watch Part Two,
Because logic's dead—and I am too.
It's fear, it's screams, it's sweaty fun—
Horror fans? We're all unwell, hon.

25. Summer Holidays

Oh sweet, sweet summer, my old flame,
Back when days were long and mostly game.
No emails, clocks, or "quick catch-ups"—
Just sunburn, sand, and soda cups.
We woke up late, then snacked for hours,
Turned sprinklers into jungle showers.
Shoes were optional, naps were banned—
And bedtime? A vague, mythical command.
Bike rides ruled, the ice cream truck sang,
We'd chase it like a sugar gang.
We built forts, got dirt on our face,
And somehow still won every race.
Now summer comes with work and sweat,
Deadlines due, and traffic threats.
We book a week, then blink—it's gone,
While emails breed like lawn at dawn.
But sometimes when the sun feels right,
And someone barbecues at night—
I hear a giggle, a sprinkler's hiss...
And time-travel back to sticky bliss.

www.ingramcontent.com/pod-product-compliance
Lightning Source LLC
Chambersburg PA
CBHW070723160726
48003CB00006BA/2360